The REAL about what's going on with our money!

And how we can change it....

I0422116

Barrington Lewis

_____

Black

Insolvency

Title

Foreword

In my line of work, I've been fortunate enough to travel and consult with many Fortune 500 corporations and spend time with many decision makers in several different cities. In order to do my job well and offer essential tax advice, it is necessary to observe actual plant operations to get an idea of how corporate purchases are being used, and how manufacturing processes are implemented. I've traveled to various locations in New York, Illinois, Ohio, Kentucky, Virginia, and Florida to name a few. But frankly, in all my travels, I've noticed that there were rarely any blacks in the C-suites, or not in the higher level positions of whom I usually sit down and meet with.

Furthermore, to my dissapointment, most of the black people were not in the corporate offices but in the plant warehouse working in the most mundane, low-skilled, and low-pay positions that seemed to lead to nowhere fast. Some of them were laughing, talking loud about the upcoming weekend events, sports, etc., and they appeared to be happy. Allbeit stereotypical, a small few of them wore nice jewelry and drove nice cars with expensive rims and nice sound systems – they appeared to be well off. I could go on but…I hope I am painting a picture for you.

So in the midst of my consulting duties I thought to myself, "How can my people afford such extravagant purchases while working in the lowest paid positions within the company?" Did they understand the positions they were in? Did they even care? Were they *really* happy? Why won't they stop spending their paychecks on bling, and instead put their paychecks in the bank?

Frankly, I don't think that most of us completely understand the positions that we put ourselves in when it comes to money. Most of us don't understand that the devaluation of the dollar over time means that we will not be able to save as much as our grandparents and parents may have been able to save. Social Security, Medicare, WIC, and any other government program will not be enough to rely on in retirement – which means that some of us will have to work past retirement age to supplement our income or possibly keep working until death.

We are responsible for our future and there will not be any one to blame but ourselves should we not be able to retire in most cases. So we must invest and attain real assets and businesses, be aggressive in making money, and constantly improve our cash flow (which is the most important aspect of retiring comfortably). We should not depend and rely on any government "social" program to be around in the future for us. Although blacks spend about the same as other ethnic groups with similar incomes, but nonetheless, it is **how** we spend – or our spending habits that are detrimental to us in the future.

This is why I wrote this book – because we need to spend our money on things that matter, get out of debt, invest, and put our money to work for us so we can become financially responsible and in control of our life. No more spending our money on Ralph Lauren, rims, eating out at restaurants, sound systems, expensive shoes, nor any other overpriced nonsense.

The United States, although a great country, accumulated much of its wealth through the use of free labor – or in other words, through the use of slaves. Because our ancestors helped to build this country and were paid little to nothing – it is our responsibility to take advantage of the opportunity they have created for us. Our ancestors would be disappointed to know that our money is being spent buying frivolous items and not accumulating any wealth for ourselves, our future, or building up our communities.

The United States' economy is primarily composed of consumer spending (almost 70%) – if blacks are spending all of our hard earned money and not accumulating any wealth, then some of us are in the same position as our ancestors! Still working hard, and not having any money. This is what **Black Insolvency** is all about. We must reverse this trend, this stereotype, if we expect to leave something behind for the next generation besides debt and financial miseducation.

This of course is not directed at ALL Blacks in America, we are not the only ethnic group that spends frivolously on unnecessary items – but since we **do** have those of us that participate in this sort of behavior, then we who are looking for change can follow the guidelines within this book to get on the right course of becoming wealthy. It is not difficult to achieve wealth and success, but there are rules to follow and perhaps a few lifestyle changes to make.

For example, if you take a look at the athletes in the sports arena, they're always training in the off season, studying videos of other athletes to see what they're doing **differently**, and constantly practicing their sport to become better at their position. And likewise, if you want to play a sport, say basketball, then you begin observing the **best** basketball players and what they do on the court – so in time, you'll start practicing and become good enough to eventually compete in the sport...or become the best to ever play the game.

Therefore, just like athletes playing the game of basketball – there are athletes playing the game of *wealth*. So if you want to play the game of wealth, then **study** the wealthiest people on the planet, **learn** how they accumulated their wealth, and find out how they are able to get even wealthier as time goes on. Practice makes perfect – so once you learn how the wealthy play the game – then **practice** investing, saving, reducing debts, until you take control of your spending habits and be a player in the game of wealth!

I hope you enjoy.

This page intentionally left blank...

Chapter 1

Income and health

The rising costs of benefits in the United States are forcing employers to push more of the costs onto their employees. This becomes more of a burden and also a wake up call for employees who rely on their employer to provide or subsidize their health insurance, 401k plan, and/or pension plan.

In the past, employees could expect to work for their employer until they retired; and when that employee decided to retire –

he/she could rely on some retirement or pension plan that was provided by their employer and/or social security that would last them throughout their retirement.

Nowadays, the employee/employer relationship is changing because most employers are now looking for ways to downsize and cut costs to become more competitive with small businesses as well as on a global level. Stated in an article from Bloomberg:

> U.S. companies are cutting back matching contributions to employee retirement plans to save cash, and the trend is growing, according to a survey by Spectrem Group.

> The survey of 150 U.S. companies found that 34 percent have reduced or eliminated retirement-plan contributions since January 2008. In the next 12 months, 29 percent intend to scale back or eliminate

their match, the survey showed. *Bloomberg 2008*

Costs for healthcare alone has been on the rise about 9% annually – which is a little more than twice the rate of inflation. So employers are faced with two options:

1. Pass costs on to employees
2. Reduce number of new hires and lower starting salaries
3. Cut down on pay raises and bonuses

As costs increase, employees are taking on part-time or odd jobs in order to increase their income so that their households are less affected with the increase. With more households taking on increased healthcare and 401k costs, I imagine the impact must really be felt amongst single-parent households. The single parent has to decide whether he/she can afford picking up another form of employment and finding a babysitter...or just taking on the risks of not having health insurance for their households until more money somehow comes in.

And since we know more black families choose to spend less on health insurance or opt out of it altogether – the room for disaster becomes just that much greater. Healthcare is a major concern in the black community because we tend to spend the less on it, although we suffer the greatest from the lack of it.

"From the cradle to the grave, racial and ethnic minorities suffer from shorter life spans, higher rates of disease and disability, and higher mortality relative to national averages." *The Louisiana Weekly*

Nevertheless, healthcare is becoming very expensive and the costs are going up every year at over twice the rate of inflation. Generally speaking, blacks, who make the least amount of money – tend to suffer the greatest compared to any other ethnic group. In the unlucky event of a health emergency, we are the least prepared to deal with our health issues if and when they arise...which unfortunately means that we are one emergency from becoming bankrupt.

Furthermore, The Centers for Disease Control and Prevention (CDC) states that blacks are the highest risk ethnic group than any other given the epidemic of AIDS cases reported.

Race or Ethnicity	Estimated # of AIDS Cases in 2007	Cumulative Estimated # of AIDS Cases, Through 2007*
American Indian/Alaska Native	158	3,492
Asian[a]	475	7,511
Black/African American	17,507	426,003
Hispanic/Latino[b]	6,921	169,138
Native Hawaiian/Other Pacific Islander	76	721
White	10,407	404,465

*Includes persons with a diagnosis of AIDS from the beginning of the epidemic through 2007.

These statistics are astounding given that Blacks/African Americans make up about 12% of the entire United States population – yet we make up 40% of all AIDS cases in the United States. Black women should have the highest cause for alarm since they make up for more than 61% of all the new cases reported in the US.

These statistics contribute to black insolvency within our community because 64% of black families are single-parent households. One parent = one income, so I imagine some of these single-parent households can slip closer to poverty if or when the sole income provider falls prey to AIDS or HIV. Since we have one of the lowest incomes compared to other ethnic groups, think of the burden it must be when we must budget for pills, shots, and other medicines in order to live if we become infected with HIV/AIDS.

Unfortunately, not enough money is spent to prevent and combat the spread of the disease within our community. It seems almost as if the largest percentage of healthcare profits are collected within our community given that we have the highest risk for diabetes, heart diseases, and STDs such as HIV/AIDS. But then again, every other rap and hip hop song on the radio talks about sex directly or metaphorically and not enough about any other event that happens on the planet...just sex, sex, and more sex music.

The word needs to get out more about the epidemic of diseases within our community and the huge profits being collected by medical providers on the black community.

Because we make the least amount of money, one can assume that we also have the least amount of **savings** as well compared to other ethnic groups to cover emergencies.

"According to Target Market, a company that tracks black consumer spending, blacks spend a significant amount of their income on depreciable products.... [Blacks] spent $22.9 billion on clothes, $3.2 billion on electronics and $11.6 billion on furniture to put into homes that, in many cases, were rented."

For Black America to have such great spending power, we sure tend to spend it on nothingness – or items that have no value. It is a shame that we spend more money on looking good than we do to better ourselves so that we may live longer. Not to mention that our eating habits and food choices are not the best, this partially explains the high rates of diabetes and heart disease amongst so many of us.

Obviously not a big secret, but "among our favorite purchases are cars and liquor. Blacks make up only 12% of the U.S. population, yet account for 30% of the country's Scotch consumption. Detroit, which is 80% black, is the world's No. 1 market for Cognac." (USA Today)

This is partially what Black Insolvency is all about – we won't get ahead to live a healthy and low stress life if we keep following the same poor choice pattern. Spending our money on unnecessary items that ultimately have no value makes us insolvent in the process.

This is why many of us don't have much to pass on to the next generation besides debt and grief. And the lack of knowledge about finances, health, and debt plagues our future if we don't start spreading good knowledge and awareness in the same manner Dr. Martin L. King, Jr. did for black equality.

Let's not live our lives **ready to die** – but rather let's live our lives to the fullest that we possibly can. Let's stop spending money on frivolous items that make us insolvent such as expensive cars, rims, expensive clothes, and jewelry, etc. Instead let's start spending our money on things that last – such as land, real estate, businesses, etc. This is how money is made and kept for generations to come.

Employers are pushing back on healthcare because it is becoming too costly for them to keep it as a tool for recruiting new talent:

> The majority of people with health insurance, about 160 million Americans, receive it through their jobs. "American families with employer-based coverage were worse off in 2007 than they were in 2004," said Jon Gabel, lead author of the study that was published in a June 2 Health Affairs Web exclusive. "This is during a period of time when the economy was expanding."
>
> The authors conclude that a growing number of people are underinsured, a term that refers only to what they

pay out of pocket for medical services. Health-care affordability, which includes out-of-pocket costs plus employees' premium contributions, also has taken a big hit. *Marketwatch 2009*

Makes one wonder sometimes if instead of overhauling a massive expense such as universal healthcare – would the private industry be able to offer something much more affordable and feasible than the government ever could? Only time will tell. But if there could be a way to eliminate pre-existing conditions (maybe with a few limitations), and at the same time put a cap on the rate of increase for health insurance – without having too much politics involved – then maybe the government could be on to something.

Too many of us continue to rely on our employer far too much and believe that because we have a job in the good times – we will have a job in the bad times. However, as each economic downturn has showed us, for some reason there always are more black people unemployed than any other ethnic group. Why is that? Additionally, when we are fired from an employer we are the largest ethnic group filing for unemployment benefits! You may say this is coincidental – but I think otherwise.

So when there is a downturn in the economy, such as this one in 2009, the President (in this case President Obama) keeps extending the unemployment benefits time and time again – which extends unemployment because people tend to continue living their life as if they are employed – when they are really just relying on government benefits.

Who pays the bill for unemployment benefits and increased social programs such as WIC, Social Security, Medicare? Well, everyone has to pay the bill eventually! Because when the government expands anything it will have to raise taxes in order to pay for these programs. And usually a democratic government raises taxes on the rich first, and then must expand its base to the middle class, then the poor.

Of course, there are families who do need assistance and we should help them – but the more government is involved, the more opportunity there is for fraud and mismanagement. Given the severely underfunded programs of Social Security and Medicare, it's questionable if the government is capable or qualified in accurately managing social programs.

The downside of social programs – besides inevitable increased taxes for all – is that the ease of access to these programs makes way for *mindless* individuals that inanely work for their employer for several years without much motivation for aspiration. And if the day comes when we are to be terminated from our jobs – we know our faithful government will be there to help keep us afloat because we have a safety net called "unemployment benefits".

Knowing that the government will always be there to "catch you if you fall" can *possibly* make some of us weak and not willing to take responsibility or give us enough motivation to keep working and be innovative enough to prevent from falling in the first place. Hell, some of us can decide to live out our lives on the government social programs and never really work again (*almost seems like a nice deal*) if you are ok to live in section 8 housing, welfare, etc., and make the least amount of money.

This is simple business economics – as employers incur high expenses and/or are taxed more, the more costs and expenses they incidentally pass onto their employees. By passing on higher costs and expenses to employees – employers can continue to keep the business' operations going and keep their best employees employed.

Most of the time when businesses have to cut costs, usually they start from the bottom up...and in most cases blacks hold these bottom positions and unfortunately are sometimes the first to be let go.

But the future holds promise for us in the arena of education....recent data shows that although blacks lag behind all other ethnic groups – the tide is slowly turning for the better. With more of us graduating from high school, going to college, and becoming productive.

Some interesting viewpoints can be made from data collected by the US Census Bureau:

Education

Note: 2006 and 2007 data in this section pertain to single-race blacks.

- **82%** - Among single-race blacks 25 and older, the proportion who had at least a high school diploma in 2007.

- **19%** - Percentage of single-race blacks 25 and older who had a bachelor's degree or higher in 2007.
- **1.2million** - Among single-race blacks 25 and older, the number who had an advanced degree in 2007 (e.g., master's, doctorate, medical or law). In 1997, 717,000 blacks had this level of education.
- **2.3million** - Number of single-race black college students in fall 2006. This was an increase of roughly 1 million from 15 years earlier.

However, when it comes to money, family, and homeownership – the future becomes a little bleak for us. Meaning that we are educating ourselves – but we are not yet implementing that education for our own good.

More data from the US Census Bureau is as follows:

Income, Poverty and Health Insurance

- **$33,916** - The annual median income of single-race black households in 2007, up from $32,876 (in 2007 constant dollars) in 2006.
- **$36,068 & $31,009** - The 2007 median earnings of single-race black men and women, respectively, 15 and older who worked full time, year-round.
- **24.5%** - Poverty rate in 2007 for single-race blacks, statistically unchanged from 2006.
- **19.5%** - The percentage of single-race blacks lacking health insurance in 2007, down from 20.5 percent in 2006.

Families and Children

- **64%** - Percentage of families among households with a single-race black householder. There were 8.5 million black family households.
- **45%** - Among families with single-race black householders, the percentage that are married couples.
- **1.2 million** - Number of single-race black grandparents living with their own grandchildren younger than 18. Of this number, 50 percent were also responsible for their care.

Homeowership – the American Dream

- **46%** - Nationally, the percentage of households with a householder who is single-race black who lived in owner-occupied homes. The rate was higher in certain states, such as Mississippi, where it reached 59 percent.

Jobs

- **27%** - The percentage of single-race blacks 16 and older who work in management, professional and related occupations. There are 49,730 black physicians and surgeons, 70,620 postsecondary teachers, 49,050 lawyers, and 57,720 chief executives.

This data from the US Census Bureau is appalling and disturbing because there needs to be great changes in our family lifestyles and income. This change is necessary in order for blacks to retire wealthy and pass on wealth to our future generations to become better suited and prepared for the future on a global basis.

As previously stated, black families are predominantly composed of one parent households (64%), which is part of the reason for our households to have lower incomes compared to other ethnic groups, because it's just one income provider as opposed to two. However, you would think that we would be better savers instead of being one of the highest spenders.

Perhaps our broken family composition is due to a damaged psyche or low self esteem within our race. We self-destruct daily. If you turn on any hiphop/rap station today, there is nothing but garbage and filth pouring into the streets of our communities. Belittling our beautiful women to hoes, bitches, and portraying them as prostitutes who have nothing better going for them besides what's between their legs.

Today's music is packed with so much violence and explicit content - it is amazing that the FCC allows it to be played over the airwaves. But, as long as it has a nice beat to it, we're bobbing our heads to it like idiots without ever taking a second to listen to the lyrics. It's no wonder our kids and teenagers want to have the latest fashions and feel they need to "shine", "floss", and "stunt", etc., because it's all they ever hear on the radio...and they want to be and dress just like their music icons.

I'm not saying all hiphop and rap is bad – just just 90% of it. We should have music that sounds good and is also uplifting and encouraging. And not the type of music that talks about violence, drugs, sex, and degrades women and men.

As of this writing the unemployment rate of blacks is hovering around 30% - although most of the country has a 10% unemployment rate. We're silently struggling.

Men step up. Women step up. We are not going to leave a bad legacy for the next generation. Sit down with your kids and teach them about what's really going on in the world and how they need to be even more competitive than ever before, because there is a need for them to compete globally.

Chapter 2

Black Churches and Wealth

One offering, two offerings, three offerings, four! Benevolent offering, Congressional offering, tithes, and more....

"Giving in Jesus name" is what we hear preached from the pulpit in almost any black church, in almost every religious denomination.   Many of us religiously give/donate our money to our church in some form or another, whether it be through offering, tithes, or some type of building fund/fundraiser – we give regardless if we can afford to or not. We give 10% of our salary for tithes, plus we participate in other offerings/funds at least once a week – so the total dollar amount we *actually* give annually can be astounding when you add it all up.

For example, take an average family's salary of $40,000 after taxes and subtract 10% for tithes right off the top (*This family is paying $4,000 annually in tithes alone!*). Now subtract another (let's say) 5% for any other miscellaneous funds and offerings we participate in. This leaves this average family with only a net income of $34,000 to cover their bills, food, and other expenses.

So if this family is one of the many black families that has a car note, credit card debt, low savings, no property, and spends their money frivolously – imagine how unwise it may be to give $6,000 of your income to the church? Especially when this family could be using that $6,000 to pay off their car note, or pay off their credit cards, and perhaps build savings.

Now I'm not trying to tell anyone not to pay their tithes and offerings (don't want to get in that hot water), but would it not make sense to get your finances on a solid ground before you go giving it all away? Some people think so – others may not.

Many people still will give to their church although they themselves are in need of money. I can't tell you of the countless times I've heard testimonies of black insolvent people in church telling stories of how they had a rent bill due, or lights were cut off, and somehow they miraculously got a check in the mail or received a "blessed handshake" just in time to pay their bill that month.

But what about next month? Are these people expecting the same "miracle" to happen to them again? Even though they are giving their money away to keep the lights on at the church? When they need to keep the lights on at their own house? This makes no sense to me.

Black Americans are in many ways the most religious people in America. Some 82 percent of blacks (versus 67 percent of whites) are church members; 82 percent of blacks (versus 55 percent of whites) say that religion is "very important in their life." Eighty-six percent of blacks (versus 60 percent of whites) believe that religion "can answer all or most of today's problems."

And the religious faith of black Americans issues today, as it has for more than a century, [is] active work in the community. In his 1899 classic, *The Philadelphia Negro: A Social Study*, W.E.B. DuBois observed, "Without wholly conscious effort the Negro church has become a centre of social intercourse to a degree unknown in white churches...." Brookings Institute 1999

Don't get me wrong – I do believe God is in the blessing business and all that – but I can't help but to believe that God has given us the power to do all things...including paying our own bills! So forgive me for saying that some church members aren't in need of prayer or a miracle, they are just in need of a well taught course in Personal Finance, Accounting, and perhaps some Economics wouldn't hurt either.

When more black people become financially literate, and stop blaming others for their own problems – I bet there will be many more prosperous black churches around that actually did a lot more in their communities than just have a prayer meeting. However, if the leaders of a church are financially illiterate, then the majority of the congregation of that church must also be financially illiterate – which explains why many of our churches remain in a storefront setting, and/or they continually struggle to get by or go bankrupt.

Black churches take in billions of dollars annually, which therefore raises the question – what are they doing with the money? Where is the improvement in the communities they serve? An interesting research study posted in BNET Today read as follows:

A groundbreaking study of U.S. black churches has found that many are suffering from financial challenges and that congregations in denominations that emphasize tithing tend to have some of the most generous donors. Walter Collier, lead researcher for the study by the Interdenominational Theological Center in Atlanta, said congregants' concern about church management of finances may prove to be a "wake-up call" for pastors. "While they [congregants] go to church on

Sunday ... for the purposes of being spiritually comforted and satisfied, they are equally concerned about how their churches manage money," he said.

Churches should be held accountable for the way it manages the money that is being given or donated to its cause. The same principle that applies to one's HOA (Home Owners Association) should apply to the Church. Similar to how home owners of an HOA should know exactly how the Board of Directors/Management is handling the money/dues it collects...and they should know whether or not the Board of Directors are *effective* and *efficient* in handling the money by requiring the Board to make available a budget and balance sheet for all home owners.

The church should **also** present the congregation with a budget and balance sheet to inform their members of how the money is being managed. This way members won't be shocked as to why the church all of a sudden needs money for equipment, repairs, or to keep the lights on. The research study from BNET Today continues below:

> The two-year study found that 54 percent of church members reported that their church was having serious financial problems. In Collier's view, the "worrisome finding," based in most cases on members' knowledge of regular church financial reports, does not bode well for churches that might be called on to help communities affected by changes in welfare legislation and reduced government funding of social services. "There's a really important need for pastors to review their stewardship practices and also think of ... ways to generate funds," he said.

It's not a wonder why state authorities have taken up the slack for members when they audit these churches that have no intent but to steal from its members. Should preachers/pastors of a church be allowed to have jets, mansions, expensive cars when the majority of their congregation suffers? Are we so blinded to follow "a man/woman of God" that we do not use our own common sense that our parents gave us?

Sadly, there are individuals who will steal from anyone in the name of God – so we need to be watchful. However, if there is no balance sheet or budget to "check the books" of our churches, then how could we know when we're being duped?

Nobody would invest in a company without doing some research and due diligence by checking the books of that company before sinking dollars into it.

Consider the church as a company as well as a place of worship, where you invest time and money...and not just a place of worship.

The church is (in a way) a company because it has to report its income to the IRS – like any other company, file tax returns – like any other company, and it also has property/equipment/sales – LIKE ANY OTHER COMPANY! We, the members, are the shareholders of this company that happens to be a church.

We invest our money into our church company, and we expect our church company to operate efficiently and not to mismanage our money – which is why we should push for our churches to make available for its members a budget and balance sheet every year.

The survey also found that black churchgoers are committed to giving to their churches. "African-Americans tend to give primarily in obedience to the covenant ... with God to tithe and to do whatever's necessary to keep the church going so that it can carry out its mission," said Collier, a social scientist and marketing researcher based in Alexandria, Virginia. Members with household incomes between $10,000 and $60,000 were found to tithe and give offerings more than people in other income groups.

In a related finding, the researchers discovered that churches generate more money when they use pledge cards to determine worshipers' intentions for annual donations. "It seems to have an effect of binding the individual, kind of getting the individual to commit," said Collier. "Once the individual writes this

down, it kind of holds him or her to
it."

Tithing is absolutely important if the
church is fulfilling its obligations, enhancing
its community, in an effective and efficient
manner. However, shouldn't we also hold
our church accountable and require that they
produce a report or summary of how the
money is being spent?

People say "a fool and his money will
soon part", this saying, although not a
scripture, has some truth to it.
The research study states in closing:

Despite the concerns about financial
matters and infrastructure, the
researchers found a great deal of
satisfaction with other aspects of
church life--including sermons,
biblical instruction and the quality of
the choirs. Commented Collier:
"Their spiritual needs are satisfied,

their need for fellowship with other people is satisfied and, given the racial climate in the country, outside of a person's individual household or home, the church is one place where you can go to and you can feel comfortable."

But spiritual comfort notwithstanding, the study also indicates that there is work to be done in the training of church leaders.

"Certainly what it shows us is that we need to be doing more in terms of training church leaders, and we need to be doing more in terms of training seminarians so that when they come out, not only are they well [prepared] in terms of scripture and church history and hermeneutics but also how to run an organization efficiently," Collier said.

Chapter 3

YOU are responsible for YOU

Everyone wants to be rich and have some bling, right? We all want to just be successful in life and have a nice house, a nice car, and money in the bank. Some of us want to go a step further, and acquire property, businesses, and wealth, to be able to pass on this fortune for generations to come so our entire family can be comfortable (just like Henry Ford when he started Ford Motor Company... and we know how long that company has been around!). After all, this is mostly what the American dream is about – where one can achieve his or her dream if they so desire and are willing to work for it.

Well, the wealth we all dream of does not come overnight, especially the wealth that sticks around for generations – achieving wealth takes vision, smart work, confidence, and persistence. Most people who achieve wealth decide that they are not going to work 8-10 hours in a cubicle everyday for the rest of their life, or in a warehouse making minimum wage, or in a job/career that they hate. They decide not answer to a boss or manager or seek permission about taking time off for vacation, about how long they can take off for maternity leave, or stress out about how many hours of sick or disability time they can use before they get fired.

Who wants to work in a job that we have no desire for? Or spend thousands of hours of our life in a job we hate and it does not pay us enough? JOB stands for Just Over Broke – so if we want to achieve wealth we must begin with your end in mind – that means we must envision where we are going to be in 10-20-30-and even 40 years from now. If our current path is not leading us to our goals including our financial security, then we must change or alter our course so that we will reach those goals. Since the dollar continues to decline in value and there is no way Social Security and Medicare will be worth anything to us once we retire – we have to be a bit more financially savvy than our grandparents and/or parents.

In college there is a saying that my counselors and professors would say to the class in order to convey the amount of studying and hard work the students would have to do in order to be successful in the course. They said:

IF you want an F in this course – aim for nothing.

IF you want a D in this course – aim for a C

IF you want a C in this course – aim for a B

IF you want a B in this course – aim for an A

IF you want an A – then you better aim higher than anyone else, cause I hardly ever give out A's!

For most of us – nobody in our lifetime is going to willingly GIVE us anything worth something, we have to EARN it. In my classes only about 10% of the students ever received A's, so that meant the other 90% of us had to settle for the rest of the grades. So to transform this scenario into dollars – if you want a million dollars, aim for 5 million dollars! If you want $5 million, then aim for $10 million. The top 10% of the world's wealth aim for hundreds of millions or even billions of dollars, and the other 90% of us have to settle for the remaining amount of dollars left. The moral of this story is to always aim higher so you will never fall short of what you're hoping to accomplish.

Of course it will be difficult and sometimes overwhelming to reach success, but it will always be worth it, even when you fail because you learn what not to do in the future. If attaining wealth and success were easy then everyone would be wealthy, rich, and successful on their first attempt. But reaching a level of success requires that you work smarter than the next person in order to achieve what you want.

So do you want to be a winner or a loser? I'm assuming you want to be a winner because you are reading this book. The reason why some African Americans do not reach their goals is because we are not sure of how to start, and a few of us have lost hope so we spend our money on anything and do not consider saving and investing that money. We instead waste all of our money on what we want today and do not consider our needs for tomorrow. Tell me, how can an ethnic group that is the lowest on the income totem pole spend the most money on unnecessary purchases than other ethnic groups???

In researching the spending habits of several ethnic groups, I came across a study that proved quite interesting on "Conspicous

Consumption and Race" conducted by University of Chicago economists Kerwin Kofi Charles and Erik Hurst. Their research suggests:

> "Using nationally representative data on consumption, we show that Blacks and Hispancis devote larger shares of their expenditure bundles to visible goods (clothing, jewelry, and cars) than do comparable Whites."

Ask yourself, if we spend most of our money on unnecessary items (or depreciating assets) then how do we expect to get ahead in life? How do we expect to save our money and buy assets that appreciate if we are wasting money on depreciating items such as clothing, jewelry, and cars? We hold **ourselves** back from attaining wealth, or from being self-sufficient entrepreneurs that do not depend on a paycheck from an employer. The study goes on to suggest:

"Holding lifetime resources constant, an increased propensity to spend on visible goods must necessarily mean lower consumption on other goods. We show that the Black-White gaps in education and health care spending (conditional on permanent income and other demographics) decline by 25 and 8 percentage points, respectively, after controlling for the share of spending allocated to visible goods.

Given that the racial gap in visible spending falls with age, there is reason to believe that wealth accumulation could be affected by spending on visible goods. To this end, we show that wealth gap between Blacks and Whites, conditional on permanent income, declines by 50 percent after controlling for visible spending."

Whatever our goals may be, I can guarantee you that we will not be able to reach them in a timely fashion if we do not begin to change our poor spending habits and educate ourselves on personal finance and investing. Instead of wasting money on all the bling, put it in the bank until you have an emergency fund established (which is normally 8-12 months of your living expenses) and invest the rest in the stock market, in businesses, and other assets so it will grow exponentially.

This study conducted by economists Charles and Hurst indicate that we spend less money on education and health care but more on clothing, jewelry, cars, and even housing in an attempt to show off or give an impression of our wealth and success or lack thereof.

As the study suggests, our consumption of "visible" goods has caused our decline in spending and investing within other areas such as education and health care. This says to me that we are undereducated and not as healthy as we could be – but we drive some nice cars and we sure do look good with our new clothes, jewelry, and/or shoes! Bill Cosby himself has continued to speak out against the poor spending habits and consumption within the Black community and is an avid supporter of Blacks becoming more focused on things that matter, such as, a decent education.

"A few years ago, Bill Cosby set off a firestorm with a speech excoriating his fellow African-Americans for, among other things, buying $500 sneakers instead of educational toys for their children. In a recent book, *Come On People*, he repeats his argument that black Americans spend too much money on designer clothes and fancy cars, and don't invest sufficiently in their futures." – *Fisman, R.*

Mr. Cosby is absolutely correct in his acknowledment of the poor spending habits of Blacks in America; therefore in this day and time we can only blame ourselves for our downfall and lack of preparation of the future. Given this behavior, we soon recognize that we become left behind due to our rambunctious spending and the desire of appearing to be wealthy or displaying a status of well-being.

One can't help but wonder if whether this spending behavior is tied to Blacks' recent political preference of one party over another – the Democratic Party. In general, the Democratic Party favors a higher minimum wage for the working class but also increased taxes to fund more social programs such as Welfare, Social Security, and Medicare. Because blacks tend to spend more frivolously than our white counterparts – one can't help but ask if we overuse these government programs as a catch-all for some of us to rely on when we eventually run out of money and can't pay bills.

Although blacks make more money in the U.S. than ever before – instead of increasing our wealth and providing a higher standard of living for generations to come – we tend to spend more money in the U.S.

than ever before. The purchasing power of African Americans/Blacks is estimated to be at $1.2 trillion by 2013 according to the University of Georgia's Selig Center for Economic Growth. This means that Blacks are a pertinent factor in consumer spending within the U.S. which accounts for 70% of overall economic activity.

As it was necessary for our ancestors to work and provide free labor to increase the wealth of others – I wonder how important is it to us, now with our freedom, to continue providing wealth for others by spending all of our money on purchases that do not increase OUR bottom line? If we spend more as we increase our incomes – we are not creating any wealth. And therefore are in the same positions similar to our ancestors that never had much...although they were forced to do so. What's our excuse? There is none.

Not all Blacks, in history and today, have negately spent their money on unnecessary items. In fact, not too long after the abolishment of slavery there were wealthy black individuals that owned land, businesses, and created wealth for their families for generations that still enjoy that foundation of wealth started decades ago. One cannot forget about our Madame C.J. Walker, George Washington Carver, and Booker T. Washington who overcame the odds against them to accomplish what they set out for.

What we can learn from these ancestors about our spending habits is to invest in our education, our community, and not to blame others for our situation, failures, and/or lack of money. If you are not happy with your situation, then you can change it. We have the power to change anything once we dedicate ourselves and put our mind to it.

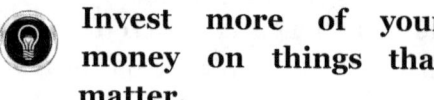 **Invest more of your money on things that matter.**

Things that matter are buying stocks and bonds or investing in businesses or franchises that have potential for a nice return on your money. After you've built up your emergency fund in the bank account – invest the rest of your money in the stock market because your money grows slowly in a bank account. The average savings rate of an online bank is about 4.5%, but the rate of inflation is about 4% annually, so this means your money in your bank account grows by 0.5% net of inflation.

One may ask, "why not put all my money in the stock market since my return will be so small in a bank account?" The answer is that a bank account is a very safe and liquid investment, and is also insured up to $250,000 by the FDIC. The money you put in the stock market is not insured at all, which makes it more risky but also means you get a higher return (more risk = more reward).

So next time when you're looking at that new SUV, those new Jordans, video game system, etc., ask yourself whether your money could be put to better use.

A friend of mine asked me about advice on how to get in the stock market and said that he would be able to invest once he paid some bills and saved a little more money in his bank account. I told him that when he is ready we can talk then – it was no use of giving out information about investing if he was not ready to play the game.

So about a month passed and my friend calls me about a vacation package he purchased and wanted to know if I would be traveling soon. I told him not right away, but I asked if he was ready to learn about how to invest and have his money work for him – instead of working for money – and he said he was not ready yet. So I went a step further and asked how much did he spend on his vacation package, he replied $500. I told him how I just spent $500 on an option in the stock market and the price rose to $1270, making me over $700 profit.

I told him this is how my money works for me, I took $500 and turned it into $1270 and was able to put my original $500 back in my bank account plus have $700 to spend, save, or invest as I pleased. He used money from his savings to spend on a vacation package that did not produce any money for him. So this transaction on my financial balance sheet was as follows:

Barrington

Savings------------------------------ **($500)**

Investment gains (loss) ------------**$1270**

[770 profit + $500 original investment]

And as I closed my position (sold) on my investment, I put my original $500 back into my savings account and used my profits as I pleased:

Savings----------------------------- **+ $500**

Profits(loss)-------------------------- **$770**

But as for my friend, his transaction on his financial balance sheet was as follows:

<u>Friend</u>

Savings------------------------------- **($500)**

Vacation package------------------- **$0**

Profits (loss)----------------------- **($500)**

This is a small example so we can clearly see the differences in these transactions – one where I used my money to work for me to make more money, and the other where my friend used his hard earned money to purchase a vacation package. If he would've followed the same principle I used he would have been able to purchase his vacation package without using any of HIS own money – instead he would've had $770 to buy his $500 package and still have $270 left over to reinvest in the market.

The smarter we become about money – the less dependent we are of government social programs. We won't make it in retirement given our rate of unnecessary spending and we can not rely on the "social programs" provided by the government as they quickly become obsolete and the standards for qualification are constantly raised. The government realizes that if it is not strict on the requirements to qualify for these programs then more people, of all races and ethnic backgrounds, will take advantage of all the Welfare, Social Security, and Medicare provided – if this happens it will destroy the entire US economy by increasing our taxes astronomically.

In reasoning, the continued and increasing use of these social programs cost our government billions of dollars and possibly trillions; however, the government's money comes primarily from taxes. Therefore as these social programs continue to exist and some individuals keep abusing them, then the bill for supporting these programs will become increasingly larger – which means the government must consistently raise taxes!

And when the government raises taxes it means that we who do not rely on these government programs will eventually work harder for less money! Can you imagine if 30-40% of your paycheck went to taxes to support those who abuse the social programs provided by the government? I bet you would not be as motivated to go to work everyday.

So therefore, the government must be strict on the requirements of these social programs and may possibly eliminate them altogether to keep the US economic engine running strongly. Likewise, I doubt that these social programs will be around that much longer for us to worry about possible extremely high taxes due to our social programs because both political parties are making it difficult to qualify for these programs and/or are getting rid of them all together.

Democrats and Republicans alike see the urgency of the insolvency that looms if they do not respond quickly. Even President Clinton, a democrat, noticed the insolvency of the Welfare system and was determined to end the social program by "[signing] historic welfare legislation...that rewrites six decades of social policy, ending the federal guarantee of cash assistance to the poor and turning welfare programs over to the states." – *Washington Post*

Furthermore, the government has also taken notice about the insolvency of other programs such as Social Security – which is severely underfunded and not able to adequately provide benefits to retirees as they reach retirement age. These programs will force the government to raise taxes, default on payments, or continue pushing back the retirement age necessary to receive these benefits. The Social Security Amendment of 1983 states: *"Full retirement age (also called "normal retirement age") had been 65 for many years. However, beginning with people born in 1938 or later, that age gradually increases until it reaches 67 for people born after 1959."*

The *1983* *Social* *Security* *Amendments* *included a provision for* **raising the full retirement age beginning with people born in 1938 or later***."*

So for those of us looking or hoping to take advantage of the "social system" are going to find themselves out of luck – but this also means that we are going to be financially accountable in the future for our actions today if we do not prepare now for retirement. The amendment goes on to say that "[the] *Congress cited improvements in the health of older people and increases in average life expectancy as primary reasons for increasing the normal retirement age."*

Although Congress states that the reason for the age increase to 67 is due to "average life expectancy", one can assume the motive behind Congress' move is due to another report released by the Social Security Board of Trustees on May 12, 2009 and presented before Congress, which states:

The Social Security Board of Trustees today released its annual report on the financial health of the Social Security Trust Funds. The Trustees project that program costs will **exceed** tax revenues in 2016, **one year sooner than projected** in last year's report. The combined assets of the Old-Age and Survivors, and Disability Insurance (OASDI) Trust Funds will be **exhausted** in **2037, four years sooner than projected** last year. The **worsening** of the long-range outlook for the Social Security program is due primarily to the recent economic downturn and faster reductions in mortality than previously assumed.

Americans will soon have to come to the reality of fundamental financial reform as our lifestyle of depending on government programs in retirement such as Social

Security, Medicare, and Welfare becomes a distant memory of the past. Hopefully you can see the dire situation at hand as I do – Blacks spend more on unnecessary items and less on education and healthcare – which means we have even less money to save an emergency fund and invest. If we are not saving and investing at optimal levels – then some of us will be short-handed as our social programs become obsolete and we cannot use them as a financial crutch anymore. Which means more of us will slip below the poverty line, especially single parent households, unless we reform our spending habits and become accountable and financially responsible for our future.

In conclusion, spend your money on things that matter such as education, proper health care, saving an emergency fund, and investing in real estate and/or businesses. Also invest in index funds instead of mutual funds, and invest in stocks that pay constant dividends.

Observe your friends and associates. You may need new ones....

Our social circles also play a part in our finances –the people that you call friends and even your family will play a role and sometimes determine whether you achieve your goal of wealth and success. People closest to you are a reflection of you in some way and have an influence in your life. Therefore, if you hang around a group of people who are broke or have a poor mind, chances are that you are broke and poor just like them or soon will be. The same is true for those who cling to a group of people who are wealthy and successful, chances are that you are wealthy and successful just like them or soon will be.

Furthermore, if you surround yourself with people who are intelligent and have dreams, and are actually **doing** something to achieve those dreams instead of just *having* them, then you will find yourself doing what you must to achieve your dreams. This is simply called PEER PRESSURE and it has a huge effect on the way we think, how we act, and what we accomplish in our lives believe it or not. The old adage of "Birds of a feather flock together" and "Great minds think alike" are good examples of why we should be conscious of whom we include in our social circles.

Having friends or associates in your social circle who are broke and aren't going anywhere are detrimental to your success and goals. It's like carrying a ton of bricks up a ladder, it weighs you down considerably. Especially when they see you attempting to advance yourself and all they do is complain, make excuses, or try to hinder your progress by being pessimistic towards your goals (also known as "hating").

Sometimes these "haters" can be someone close, such as your spouse, which can make it difficult to avoid them while you work towards your goal. But if your heart is really in it, you will find a way to accomplish your goals while keeping your spouse happy and not ruining your marriage.

 Get rid of bad debt. It works against you and your goals until it is completely paid off!

In addition to reforming bad spending habits – we must also not forget to rid ourselves of bad debt. It has been said that one sleeps better at night and has less stress in life when he or she reduces their bad debts, and besides that – having less bad debt and keeping more of your money just makes sense. Matter of fact, the top 1% of wealthy families in America have a little over 7% of bad debt in their entire financial balance sheet compared to 73% of bad debt for the bottom 90% of America.

Take a look at the spreadsheet below indicating the percentage levels of the debts of each social class:

	Housing, Liquid Assets, Pension Assets, and Debt		
	Top 1 percent	Next 9 percent	Bottom 90 percent
Deposits	20.8%	40.1%	39.1%
Pension accounts	13.5%	44.8%	41.7%
Life insurance	21.4%	36.0%	42.7%
Principal residence	9.8%	28.2%	62.0%
Debt	**7.2%**	**19.9%**	**73.0%**
TOTAL	12.2%	33.5%	54.3%
From Wolff (2007).			

So if the top 1% of wealthy families in America does not have a lot of bad debt – then **why** are we in the bottom 90% holding on to bad debt? This is Rule#3 in obtaining wealth and success. So do yourself a favor and start paying down bad debts beginning with the smallest bad debt you have and working your way up until all of your bad debts are completely paid off. Dave Ramsey explains in his book "Total Money Makeover" a very simple way of paying off debts by first establishing at least a $1000 emergency fund in your bank account and then living on the bare minimums while putting forth all of your efforts and remaining money to pay off your other debts. While the $1000 savings might be a bit small for an initial emergency fund in this day and time, Ramsey's book has helped millions of people become debt free.

This can be a long process depending on how much bad debt you may or may not have – however, at least you're making progress towards your ultimate goals, which is to take control of your life and your future, get out of bad debt, and retire early. Paying off bad debts will also help you in getting out of that career that you hate so much but can't leave because you need the money. And if you're underpaid in your current position, you will free up more of your cash flow by reducing bad debts and increasing your discretionary income.

But, if you notice – I've only talked about the importance of getting rid of bad debts because they hold us down...but what about good debts? You have the ultimate choice of whether you will be transforming borrowed money into good debts or using it for bad debts. Bad debts keep you down and take money out of your pockets, such as car notes, student loans, mortgages, credit cards, etc.

Using borrowed money for the purpose of Good debts can put money into your pockets if you use it for purchases that matter, such as, owning businesses, investment properties, investing in commodities, and investing in stocks that pay good dividends. The wealthiest people in the world use good debts to increase their cash flow and take advantage of capital gains.

Poor people depend on a paycheck as their sole means of income and therefore end up searching for a higher paying job, a raise or promotion, or they have to work 2 jobs in order to keep pace with the economy. Wealthy people have multiple streams of income and have a choice of whether they want to work or retire early from their job.

Use debt to put money in your pockets, because you should always have a decent cash flow. I will discuss this in further detail later in this book.

Remember, you are ultimately responsible for you – do not rely on the government to take care of you, your retirement, your family's future, etc. Let's begin with basics of building wealth to identify the different opportunities of how most of us can achieve our dreams and success by using discipline and innovative ideas to BE FREE.

Chapter 4

Beginning with the basics....

First, on your road to wealth and success you have to start with working to obtain an up to date credit report to determine whether or not you have a good credit score if you don't know. People rich AND poor can sometimes have the most problems in life because of a bad credit history or sometimes they haven't established a long enough credit history or used enough credit – and this can keep their credit score low or not as high as it needs to be. Credit is not all bad – it is something you want to have in case of emergency...but it can also cause harm to us if we do not use it properly.

Our credit score is attached to us throughout life much in the same way that our social security number is attached to us; and therefore our lives and well-being can be constantly affected by it. Having a low credit score means that you pay more and are faced with greater difficulty than others with a higher credit score.

For instance, those with a low credit score:

1. Have to sometimes put down a higher deposit on their apartment if they decide to rent

2. Have a higher rate in interest on their mortgages, credit cards, car notes, and other loans

3. Sometimes are not able to get good employment with reputable firms that hire based on your credit score

4. Are required to put down money for utilities, landline phones, and cell phones

Chances are that if you have a lower credit score you are constantly paying more in fees and deposits, etc., instead of keeping your money for yourself or using it for other expenditures, savings, or investments. Unfortunately, living with credit is becoming more of a standard than ever before – instead of having credit for "emergency" purposes only, more people have to constantly rely on revolving credit just to make ends meet given the rate of inflation outpacing the rate of wage increases.

Minorities, however, are disproportionately represented in the U.S. amongst those who have the lowest credit scores and do not have the same access to financial services and products than those of us with high credit scores. Let's change this statistic and our credit history from good to bad and raise our scores from low to high.

Furthermore, credit continues to be an integral part of our society and is a factor that judges us on our character and/or our ability to repay loans back to creditors. Therefore, it is the reason why I list having good credit as the first basic step to BE FREE.

 Obtain a free credit report and work towards establishing good credit

If you ever want to start a business or be able to borrow other people's money to invest it in the stock market or for a franchise then you must have knowledge of your credit score and a report of your credit history. There are 3 credit reporting agencies that maintain a record of your credit history and score – the agencies are:

1. Experian

2. Equifax

3. Transunion

According to Fair Credit Reporting Act, we are eligible to receive a free credit report annually from each of these agencies at annualcreditreport.com – we can decide whether we want to receive our report from all 3 agencies up front, or we can choose 1 agency every 4 months to ensure nothing shows up on our credit report that isn't supposed to be there.

Building credit is not an easy task and it takes months, or even years, to undo mistakes of the past that may have damaged your credit score. Credit management is now an integral part of our financial life as more Americans need it to sustain their current standard of living – so having poor credit or doing without it probably means that your standard of living could be better.

Here are 3 steps to take to build your credit score up:

1. Pay all of your bills on time

2. Open up a checking/savings account

3. Never max out your credit cards or take on too much debt that you can't repay within 2-3 months

Although carrying balances on credit cards ultimately puts you at risk given that these credit card agencies can raise your interest rates without your notice – even if you're a long time customer that has always paid towards their monthly balance.

 Invest in dividend paying stocks...and get paid!

Some people are stuck in neutral – they just don't get it and probably will never get it when it comes to their own personal finance or creating wealth for the next generation. Most average American has student loans, maxed credit cards, car notes, and other miscellaneous debts that we tend to carry for decades hoping to rid ourselves free of it by the time we retire. But why do we have these debts so long? I suppose we can blame a few certain individuals with MBA's and JD's (I'm talking about politicians here) that have shaped our economy into a consumer driven one, where we are punished to save (taxed) and rewarded for debt (tax deduction).

We Americans typically work 40 to 80 hr hard work weeks and take limited vacation and use barely any sick time so that we can be at the top of the list to receive any promotion, bonus, or salary increase so that we may use the extra money to pay off some debt. Once we get ourselves a little out of debt by paying off the credit cards or the car note, then what do we do?

Instead of investing or saving our money – we simply look for another car to buy because our current one is too old or "doesn't look good anymore", or some form of jewelry, rims, etc. But if we can't buy it totally outright, we simply finance the rest. And again we're back in the same situation and working extra hard to get back out of debt again.... This is what we call the rat race.

Because we never move ahead, we just move in circles going nowhere.

Black people do not have any money because they mostly give it away to rich people. Most of us work for rich people already, but unforutnately we take our hard earned money and give it right back to them when we buy our clothes, shoes, cars, jewelry, tv's, etc. So as of 2008, I began changing the way I made and spent my money.

Most black Americans might agree that we only have one stream of income – our job and a meager 401k. But to really get ahead in life, we need multiple streams of income similar to our corporate structures. Corporations have multiple streams of income through the sale of bonds, issuance of stocks, and sales of products and services.

Therefore, my quest to build multiple streams of income is beginning, instead of paying Nike for a pair of shoes, I invest in Nike and they **pay me** a dividend so I can get a pair of shoes every quarter. Instead of paying a car company like Ford or Toyota for a new car, I invest in them so that they **pay me** a dividend and I can pay cash for a car (eventually after I save up my dividends). I actually **want** gas prices to **rise** – because that means my oil & gas companies will do better and **pay me more** in dividends so that I can fill my tank up whenever I want.

Now I am far from where I want to be and definitely don't have buckets of money running over, but I hope I'm on my way as I get older and wiser. I know the financial education we received in school has been incorrect and not sufficient in today's economy, so I'm working to improve on my situation day by day.

Why would I continuously work hard just to pay companies for their products? When they are so happy to **pay me** in dividends to use their products?

Plan for retirement...you may need more than what you think.

Is an early retirement possible for you and/or your family? How much can one expect to save if he/she regularly invests and saves their money up until their retirement? This is a serious topic because there are several sources of information telling us that if we save regularly for X amount of years then by the time we retire, we will be millionaires. But how much value will a million dollars hold by then?

I'll provide a clear example of this: Let's say that Darius Green makes $40,000 today and decides that he wants to have $1.5 million by the time he retires in 40 years from today – which would make him 68. He expects to receive an average pay raise of 6%. According to Bloomberg Retirement Calculator – If he made regular contributions and saved at least 20% of his salary annually he would accumulate a sum of $1,732,188 –

which actually exceeds his goal (excluding Social Security) by the time he is ready to retire.

Green believes that he is on track to a successful retirement if he averages an 8% return on his investments. Unfortunately, he did not consider the actual value his $1.7 million will be 40 years from today. Using TVM (time value of money), we are able to calculate how much $1.7 million is worth today to get an idea of what it would be like for Green to retire in the future.

Using the formula of TVM:

$$FV/(1+r)^T = 1,732,188/ 1.08^{40}$$

This will give us an understanding of what Green's retirement will be worth in the future – or rather what $1.7 million will be worth 40 years from now. After solving for the equation we find that Darius Green's retirement will be worth roughly $79,734 for retirement. Assuming we don't have a mortgage, credit cards, or any other bills that prevent our savings for retiremet – who can survive off of just $79k? Perhaps this is possible if Green did not have any debts by the time he retired. Imagine the lifestyle adjustment....

According to Bloomberg, Green needs to *aim higher* – and save more money in order to retire comfortably as the Time Value of Money erodes his retirement value.

How many of us can successfully retire?

 Real estate is also a good investment. Acquire a few properties to become diversified with your investments.

Just as there are opportunities in the stock market today, there are also **several opportunities** in real estate as well – where one can buy properties at a low price and invest for capital gains and/or for cash flow. But just as you eventually need an exit strategy for your investments in the stock market, you also need an exit strategy for real estate.

Take, for example, Shannon Banks who owns an investment property in the form of 2 duplexes with a value of $219,000 each, or a total of $438,000. After a down payment of $100,000, Shannon owes a total of $338,000 in loans for these properties that she bought in March 2009. Since each duplex can house 2 families each, she decides to rent out all 4 units for $700/month.

As the economy regains traction and the housing market stabilizes, it is estimated that in year 2012 the value of Shannon's duplexes will appreciate to a total of $620,000. Let's fast-forward and say it is now year 2012. Shannon owes approximately $315,000 on her property which is now valued $620,000 – which means she has approximately $305,000 of equity in her duplexes.

Let's say instead of selling her duplexes for a profit and paying fees and taxes on the sale of her investment, Shannon **refinances** to take advantage of the equity in her investment property. The bank gives her a new loan for $550,000. By refinancing, Shannon **defers** her capital gains taxes and pays off her original loan of $315,000 and pockets the $235,000. Since Shannon did not yet sell the property, she gets to defer her capital gains taxes until a later date.

So now Shannon can use her $235,000 to purchase another property that she can use to rent out and **increase** her already $2,800/month income, or she can invest this money into the stock market and not have to worry about taxes until she decides to either take her money out of the market, or decides to sell her duplexes.

This is **smart money**. Shannon is using her money to work for her, instead of her working for it! By deferring her capital gains tax to a later date – she ultimately pays less taxes.

Why? Because of the *time value of money*. If Shannon defers her taxes to 30 years from today – the **real value** of what she pays in the future will be less than if she sold her property and paid taxes today.

Work **smarter**. **Think** harder.

Chapter 5
Keys to Success

So now we know that we need to be more responsible for ourselves, and we need to invest in stocks and acquire real estate. But exactly how do we do this? Where do we start and even begin to acquire or build wealth? The keys to success are very simple and the first and most important one is patience.

Patience is the **most important** key to success because there is no "get rich quick scheme" that will give us the wealth we desire to have. If it sounds too good to be true – then it usually is! Almost every individual that has acquired great wealth or riches, excluding an inheritance, has put in several hours a day, 7 days a week of work before they get the recognition or success they dream of.

Don't quit your day job just yet – but instead of spending your extra money on a new car, shoes, or clothing, spend your money on building up a stock portfolio. Every time you get a raise, promotion, or bonus – put that extra money in some stocks or even bonds and invest for the long term. Stocks that pay a consistent dividend are going to be your best choice.

The "rat race" term comes from people who work hard and compete in the workplace for an increase in salary, and then when they get a salary increase, they spend more money by buying more expensive cars, eating out more at restaurants, etc. Therefore, they get back in the same position that they were in before receiving the salary increase.

In other words, people who **remain** in the rat race are **insane**! Albert Einstein suggested that insanity is when one does the same thing over and over again and expecting different results. Likewise, people that get an increase in salary, and then increase their expenses, never really improve their financial position. Until we become successful entrepreneurs, keep your day job and have patience by getting your steady raises/bonuses, investing in stocks/bonds, and keeping your expenses low.

However, when investing in stocks, you first need a brokerage firm such as Scottrade, Sharebuilder, and TD Ameritrade to name a few. Depending on your risk profile, you can decide to purchase individual stocks or decide whether to invest in an index fund. I say index funds instead of mutual funds because index funds usually outperform mutual funds and they don't charge you "maintenance fees". If you invest in individual stocks then you need to have the time and expertise in selecting the right stocks that match your appetite for risk.

Selecting individual stocks that pay out dividends are a good way to build up an income stream over time. Analysts suggest that buying value and small cap stocks yield the best results than other stocks.

The second key to success is to **acquire real estate**. One can invest directly in properties, or invest indirectly by investing in companies who have several properties in their portfolios – or in other words investing in a safe real estate investment, such as a REIT (Real Estate Investment Trust). Either an individual can save up for a 10% down payment on a property and get financing (with a good credit score) – or he/she can put their money into a REIT and receive a portion of that REIT's rental income proportionate to the amount you invest.

Real estate gives an individual the opportunity to purchase a foreclosure at a very cheap price, invest some capital to restore the house to living conditions, and make a significant return if or when he/she sells the property. One good thing about real estate is that it is tangible property – versus holding paper stocks of a company that could go bankrupt and destroy your investment (which is why we must diversify!).

If you own some rental property, work hard to pay off your mortgage on that property. If you can keep a tenant in your rental property on a regular basis – you will be able to keep the full rent paid to you instead of using part of the rent to pay down the mortgage. Furthermore, when your mortgage is paid off, and there is some equity within your rental property, you can take some equity out of your property as a down payment for the purchase of another rental property. As of this writing, the government allows you to do this without paying any capital gains tax until if or when you sell your rental property!

Everyday people take out home equity lines of credit (HELOC) to pay down other debts that they have accumulated over time, and then they wrap or consolidate all of these loans into their mortgage. When people apply for HELOC loans, and they're approved, the government does not require them to pay taxes on DEBT. This is weird, huh? People use HELOC loans to consolidate their student loan balance into their mortgage; they consolidate credit cards, car notes, and even home improvements. As you can see – most of the time, the government will not tax you on debt.

So think of the wealth possibilities if you were approved for a HELOC loan, and you used this credit to finance anothe rental property? You are able to use your equity in either your primary residence or through your 1st rental property to finance a 2nd or 3rd property without paying any capital gains tax.

If you sold your rental property with equity in it (in other words, you made a profit) then the government will tax you at the current capital gains tax rate.

If you have equity and decide not to sell your rental property right away:

1. You can purchase another one without paying capital gains tax
2. You will have more tenants to collect monthly rent checks from
3. You can use equity from all of your properties to buy even another rental property and not pay capital gains tax.

This is how money is made and kept. If you are a hard worker and keep your day job in addition to your rental income – you will be able to eventually pay off all of your mortgages and just watch the money really roll in.

The third key to success is a very important one as well – and requires that we do our **due diligence** and learn as much as possible about our money and about any big purchase, such as a mortgage. So many of us got taken advantage of during the "2007 credit era" because we accepted what loan officers and banks told us – and did not do our own research before signing the dotted line.

Never buy anything before you understand completely what it is you're committing yourself to...this is just **plain** and **simple** common sense. If there is something you don't understand – then keep asking questions until you do. Ask other people who have used the same lender, utilize the internet if necessary. But please do not buy before you know what you're buying. Nonetheless, the NAACP is filing a lawsuit against mortgage lenders who they believed unfairly targeted minorities. But if minorities simply chose to **not** do their own research – how can they be angry at the mortgage lenders who just saw an opportunity to profit? Although it wasn't just minorities who got duped, white people who also chose not to do their own research were unfairly targeted as well – and were soon foreclosed on as the rates on their jumbo loans soared.

The fourth and final key to success is to stop following the Joneses, pay off debts, and stop trying to keep up an image that we cannot afford. We need to stop worrying so much about wearing the most expensive and newest fashions. So much of our money is spent buying TVs, cars, jewelry, and clothing – yet our savings accounts barely rise above $3,000.

According to research provided by Ariel Capital Mgmt. and Charles Schwab:

"Blacks remain less worried about retirement despite having far less money saved in retirement accounts (the median amount saved is $59,000 for Blacks versus $93,000 for Whites). Blacks contribute less to their retirement accounts monthly (the median monthly contribution is $254 for Black employees compared to $306 for White employees). Lastly, when asked about other retirement savings outside retirement accounts, the median amount for Blacks who have such savings is $36,000, compared to $75,000 for Whites.

Blacks also have family issues that compound the gap. The survey found Blacks receive less financial support from their parents and carry heavier financial burdens related to aging parents, adult children as well as other relatives. According to the survey, 27% of Blacks versus 18% of Whites have an adult living in their home other than a spouse. Only 21% of Blacks compared to 35% of Whites have received an inheritance, and only 18% of Blacks versus 34% of Whites expect to receive one in the future."

So to make the keys to success even simpler – here is a step by step chart to follow in order to get our finances on the right path and put an end to black insolvency that has plagued us for generations.

Keys to Success: Step-by-Step

1. Have Patience
2. Invest in dividend stocks and real estate
3. Do your due diligence
4. Stop following the Joneses, and pay off debts
5. Have more than one income

Having more than one income (i.e. having more than one job) may sound crazy or unnecessary – but it is becoming a necessity as more Americans need to work even harder to pay back student loans, pay off credit card debt, and secure a retirement. Just working one job and saving a 401k is not enough money by the time you retire – unless you progress up the corporate ladder to become CEO.

Retirement is becoming an ever more distant reality because so many Americans are NOT retiring – many of us will have to work past the retirement age in order to pay medical bills and expenses because our 401k and savings aren't enough. Think about those greeters at Wal-Mart; or the elderly baggers at Publix. These unfortunate people have to get up everyday and go to work instead of maybe going fishing, or visiting grandkids, etc. The reality of **not** retiring is more possible than actually retiring.

Blacks/African Americans are more susceptible to not retiring than any other ethnic group. How sad must it be when our parents or grandparents become ill or need our support – and we can't afford to do so? Or they have some emergency and not enough cash to cover it? Do we loan them money although we ourselves aren't in a good financial position? Or do we allow our elders to rack up credit card debt? Even though they may or may not be working? This would probably be a tough choice to make.

As we know, we have not been good consituents of money – data shows that we have not been smart in saving and investing. Although we look up to them, many of us have parents that have not been good teachers of money – and when it is their time to retire – some, unfortunately, look to their kids for support. Do you tell your dad or your mom that you cannot or will not give them money? Is it your job to support your parents? Answer: NO! I know it sounds a bit insensitive – but if we are not in a sound financial position, then we need to tell our parents NO!

And vice-versa, it is not our parents' responsibility to support us once we become grown and out of their house. Once our parents retire, they have enough worries and problems to make sure their money lasts throughout their retirement – and they should not be giving their kids any big loans or large sums of cash.

Another key for success is to **stop co-signing for car notes, loans, and credit cards!** Many of us destroy our own credit scores by co-signing for loans for a close family member or friend. This is a horrible thing to do. If that person were to default on their loan – guess what? YOU have to pay for it and will get harrassing phone calls to pay up the balance of the debt. Nevertheless, people still continue to co-sign for loans although it puts them at risk for a low credit score and ruin relationships between family and friends. Do yourself a favor...Just avoid it.

I hope you find this book in good favor – I hope it becomes a wake up call for black people all over. Black Insolvency is killing us, and we need to educate ourselves properly so that we may become more efficient. Why can't we get together and form multi-million dollar corporations? We always know how to "get by" and do more with less. But does it really have to be this way for the majority of us?

Let's change it by educating ourselves. Begin with the man/woman in the mirror. Then help teach someone else. Let us improve upon the foundation that our ancestors laid for us, and not be so complacent while we are still short of the goal. And that goal is to become financially responsible, enlightened, and empowered for ourselves and the upcoming generations.

My 2009 Bio:

Barrington received his B.S. in Business Administration from Florida A&M University, and soon obtained with honors an M.B.A in Finance from South University.

Barrington has a strong passion for Finance and has always been happy to educate friends, family, and people in his community about various topics on Finance and Investing.

Constantly writing and posting to his **<u>BLOG</u>** - Barrington hopes to inform and educate others on how to BE FREE and permanently leave the rat race.

Currently, Barrington is studying for his CAIA designation.

References:

Domhoff, G.W (2005). *Who Rules America: Wealth, Income, and Power*

Wolff, E. N. (2004). *Changes in Household Wealth in the 1980s and 1990s in the U.S.* Unpublished manuscript.

Wolff, E. N. (2007). *Recent Trends in Household Wealth in the United States: Rising Debt and the Middle-Class Squeeze* Annandale-on-Hudson, NY: The Levy Economics Institute.

Kerwin, K.C., Hurst, E. (2007). *Conspicuous Consumption and Race* University of Chicago; University of Pennslyvania: Wharton School of Business

Fisman, R. (2008). *Cos and Effect*

Vobejda, B. (1996). Clinton signs welfare bill amid division

SocialSecurity.gov (1983). *The Full Retirement Age is Increasing*

The Christian Century Foundation (1998) *Finances and the Black Church.* *http://findarticles.com/p/articles/*

_mi m1058/is 36 115/ai 53542648 /_

Brookings Institute 1999: Supporting Black Churches: Faith, Outreach, and the Inner City Poor

http://www.brookings.edu/articles /1999/spring religion diiulio.aspx

Smedley, B (2009): Healthcare reform important to blacks

http://www.louisianaweekly.com/n ews.php?viewStory=1473

USA Today: Tough choices for tough times

http://www.usatoday.com/news/o pinion/editorials/2004-04-01-young x.htm

Marketwatch (2009): Out of pocket health costs up 34% in 3 years

http://www.marketwatch.com/stor y/out-of-pocket-health-costs-up-34-in-3-years

www.ingramcontent.com/pod-product-compliance
Lightning Source LLC
Chambersburg PA
CBHW060417290526
45791CB00002B/793